About the Author

As a barrel child, born in Kingston, Jamaica, I left in 1981 to join my mother in England at age thirteen. I am the eldest child of six siblings. I attended Tivoli Gardens High School in Jamaica and lived in Kingston 11. I attended Brondesbury and Kilburn High School in London and later graduated with an honours degree in Finance and Accounting at the Thames Valley University (Ealing Campus). I am a mother of four children, the youngest in his final year at high school. There were challenges to face in a new country of residence and the journey had many ups and downs. However, my own story is different as I saw my mother leave to make life better for her girls and as promised, though after five years which seemed like a lifetime (for a child), she kept her promise. Life is not easy but where failure is not an option you will make it. I can only continue to aspire to my purpose and pray at the end I will have accomplished all my goals.

To: Lee

Perlene 'Jump Out of the Frying Pan into the Fire'

Wishing you abundant success!

Sherene Rutherford

Sherene Rutherford

Perlene 'Jump Out of the Fying Pan into the Fire'

Olympia Publishers
London

www.olympiapublishers.com
OLYMPIA PAPERBACK EDITION

A CIP catalogue record for this title is
available from the British Library.

ISBN: 978-1-78830-273-9

First Published in 2019

Olympia Publishers
60 Cannon Street
London
EC4N 6NP

Printed in Great Britain

Dedication

This book being my first to be published, I dedicate to my four wonderful children Keisha, Kareem, Joshua and Samuel and my lovely mother, Lorna. I also dedicate this book to my dear friend Ian who has helped me tremendously to make this book possible. Thank you to everyone who has supported me through this journey and I hope you all enjoy its contents. I give gratitude to God for giving me the inspiration to write this book whilst going through my grieving process after losing my beloved sister Georgia.

Acknowledgements

I would like to thank Olympia Publishers for their involvement in the publication of this book and give thanks for their encouragement and diligence.

Introduction

When a child is born, the journey of life begins and it continues until the heart takes its final beat. No wonder the baby cries when it leaves the womb for as the day turns to night so must the journey start.

It was a summer's day the 31st May 1981, when the three girls boarded the British Airway flight to England to join their mother in London, England. They had not seen her since the summer of 1976 when she left Jamaica to join her mother in England.

Perlene, being the eldest, held Antoinette's hand, the youngest of the sisters, and walked up the stairs to board the aircraft ; Camille walked closely behind, not exactly sure of what to expect boarding an aircraft for the very first time. The journey was long but the flight attendant was welcoming and as all three girls were under age (the eldest being 13 years old at the time), they were cared for by the staff on board the aircraft.

They landed in London, England on 1st June and it was a beautiful sunny day. Their mother was waiting at the airport impatiently for Perlene and her sisters to arrive and you can just imagine the tears of joy from a mother who had not seen her girls for five years. The girls also saw their mother's younger brother, Tony, who was born in England and was only five years older than Perlene in age. Anrol (Perlene's mother) took care of Tony after their mother's death and so he lived with her. He drove Anrol to the airport to meet them.

Perlene's mum was even more beautiful than she had envisaged her to be. She left Jamaica when Perlene was nine years old but she remembered her well. The memory of her mother was the foundation that kept her sane and also gave her hope. Perlene's mother was a kind and loving person who always showed her love and though she would discipline her children if they did wrong, it was never done out of hate or bitterness, but love and concern.

Perlene remembered when her mum was travelling to England, she told her that she would either send for them to join her in England and if that was not possible she would return to remain with them in Jamaica. Perlene believed everything her mother told her as she never lied to her and so she had no doubt in her mind those words were true.

As a child Perlene always felt her mother's love, and most family and extended family members said that she resembled her mother. Her mother was a beautiful woman and so she felt that she was beautiful too.

In Jamaica where Perlene is from, adults usually give little thought to children's feelings. Often they will use words to describe a child without giving much thought to how it may affect them. She can remember her aunt saying that her sisters, Antoinette and Camille, were being beautiful, but they would only describe her as resembling her mother. Perlene did not know at the time that they disliked her mum because she left Perlene in her dad's care when she left for England and never returned to him. The sight of Perlene was a constant reminder, and the reason for them to describe her in that manner. However, this behaviour did not stop Perlene from loving her sisters as she naturally loved them and her mum embedded a sense of togetherness within them, so they had strong bonds.

Looking back, had Perlene not retain the memories of a loving mother who was her hero who would come and rescue her from an unhappy childhood, she may have developed bitterness in her heart even towards her sisters.

Perlene hugged her mother and the tears of joy rolled down her cheeks. She felt safe again; finally mum's promise had matured. Antoinette stared at their mother emptily. She appeared not to remember who she was; she hugged her because Camille and Perlene did so. Perlene knew that life would get better being around her guardian angel (mum) and that no harm could come to her whilst she was watching over her.

Anrol was pregnant so was looking radiant. She was soon to give birth to Lorraine and though it was a surprise to the girls, Perlene felt very happy because she loved babies and would help to spoil her; well at least so she thought.

They drove to Willesden Green where her mother lived in a maisonette (flat) and she showed them their rooms and around their new home. It was lovely and Perlene was happy and safe from the violence, the verbal abuse, sexual abuse and the beatings. God had given her a second chance but this time she hit the jackpot and God had given her back security and a loving home.

Perlene's mum gave birth to a beautiful baby girl 12 days after they arrived and she was so tiny and cute. Lorraine was loved by all and she was constantly being held by the family. The girls helped to care for Lorraine. They had another sister too who was two years old (Adole). Adole accepted her big sisters as Anrol spoke about them constantly to her and prepared her in advance for their arrival. Perlene was very family orientated and so naturally played the role of 'Big Sister' as they all had the same mother who did not show favouritism in any way. They grew accepting of each other and there was no segregation even though they did not all have the same father or the same surnames. Sure there was sibling rivalry because they were children and had their individual demands.

School in England was quite different in comparison to Jamaica and she was now in the 10th grade. Perlene did not get to choose the options she would have preferred because most children chose their options at the end of year 9 and of course she was still in Jamaica. However, the options she took were OK and she worked hard to get good grades. Camille was in year 8 and Antoinette year 7. They were soon very well known in their new school because they were known to stand up for themselves and it meant that if they got into trouble for doing so then so be it.

Perlene found the climate very different. When she arrived in England it was hot and so she had no idea of what the cold felt like or even what the snow felt like. Sure she saw snow in books she read whilst in Jamaica but had no idea of what to expect. She started school that September as it was almost the summer holidays when she arrived and she had to register for school along with her sisters, so had to go through the registration procedures and processes. Antoinette started primary school within weeks as she got through the clearing system earlier than Camille and Perlene. However, she was only there for a month or so as she started year 7 that September.

Perlene's first day at school was stressful as she did not know her way around the school and the school system was confusing to her. She had not yet made friends and did not know anyone except her siblings who were in different year groups. She now had the challenge of making friends. The children seemed quite foreign to her and her accent being of Jamaican dialect was a bit difficult for her peers to understand. It took Perlene sometime to make friends but she did as she was not shy at all.

Winter came early and so did the snow. Perlene did not feel she would survive the first winter. She padded herself up well and spent little time playing in the snow as she realise that though it looked inviting it was too cold to enjoy. As a matter of fact she noticed that after the snow came the worst bit; the black ice. This was dangerous and so she had to wear boots. The fashion was different because one had to wear a coat or freeze to death and abominable snowman boots were worn to protect their feet from chill blades and frostbite.

"Goodness, the snow was very pretty but in reality was certainly not enjoyable," said Perlene. Camille and Antoinette on the other hand got their hat, scarf and gloves on, along with their coats and padded boots and went out in the back garden to play with the snow. They made snowballs and threw them at each other and they made a snowman with the help of the children next door who were from Ireland. They were very friendly and fun to play with.

Camille was quite a popular girl and was very beautiful and so kept fighting off the boys who followed her around. However, one particular boy named Alphanso refuse to give up his pursuit and eventually Camille grew to like him and in so doing they developed an intimate relation.

Antoinette, who resembled a mixed-race child, had freckles on her face and was quite attractive. She was very aggressive when boys showed interest and so they kept their distance as she had a swift tongue and flying kicks.

Both Camille and Antoinette had their mother visiting school on various occasions because they got into trouble and though they knew she would punish them when they got home, they were prepared to suffer the consequence for their actions.

Perlene did not do well in some of her 'O' level subjects so she stayed on in 6th form for one year which proved fruitful as she managed to achieve better grades and move on to college to embark upon a BTEC course in Business Studies. She completed the course successfully within the two year duration and later went onto university and completed an honours degree in finance.

Camille

Whilst in year 11 at school Camille fell pregnant to Alphanso and had a baby boy. Alphanso and Camille rented a flat and moved in together, but life began to change for both of them when the reality of extra expense became apparent with a new baby and the fact that neither of them had sufficient education and experience to get a good job that could pay the bills and allow them to live comfortably.

Alphanso turned to the bottle for comfort and Camille got frustrated and screamed at Alphanso to find a job that could pay the bills. Eventually Alphanso went to college to learn a skill whilst Camille stayed home and cared for their son. This was not to last because Camille fell pregnant with their second child and Alphanso moved on to greener pastures as he had now become 'Prince High and Mighty', charming those that fell prey to him. Camille moved on with her life by moving house and went back to college to achieve qualifications. By so doing Camille found a good job and was able to provide financially for her children and herself.

She was ambitious and wanted a career but childhood demons started to set in which she kept hidden for many years. She began to struggle emotionally to keep sane and she did this silently for a long time.

Antoinette

Antoinette on the other hand finished school and also went on to college. She got her first job as a supervisor in Tesco's and she performed well in carrying out her task. Eventually after finishing college she got a job in finance, but also had a daughter at age 18. She moved into a flat with her partner, but she was ambitious and her partner was a dreamer. She soon realised this and moved on. She was the first of the three to buy her home and moved away from North West London to Middlesex. She did well with her life and continued progressing in her career.

Perlene

As for Perlene, she had her daughter at the age of 19 and life got tough. She broke up with her partner before the baby was born. He had a relationship with another girl and she was not going to share a man, so she stepped out of his way and raised her baby girl solely with her mother's help. She was at college when she fell pregnant but finished her course and found a job with an advertising agency. Perlene worked for two years and then decided to go to university and pursue a degree. Her mother helped her to look after her daughter whilst she studied. She had a few failed relationships before she met her husband and by then she had given birth to a baby boy. Meeting her husband was good for her because he helped her to regain self esteem and though they were separated at the beginning of their marriage because he was deported back to Jamaica for a period of three years approximately, he had been a blessing to the family.

Meeting Judas changed the direction she found herself being positioned, because of want. He was very hard working and had high but achievable goals. When they met, Perlene was living in a council flat with her two children and within a year of marriage they had found a house in Middlesex, close to her mother who was already living there for a number of years and her sister Antoinette. He helped her to pay off some of her debts so that they could be financially stable, even before he was deported back to Jamaica for overstaying in England. Overstaying, however, did not mean he did wrong; he was just unfortunate and he served the time for allegedly committing the crime.

Judas being away from her for three years was a struggle but their love kept them going and as soon as the deportation order was lifted he was back in England, the first opportunity he got to join his family. Judas sets himself goals and he achieves them and where he is unable to achieve them short term; he reschedules them for a longer term. They had two boys together adding to their family, now four children. But he counted all as his own.

Perlene Meets the Man of Her Dreams?

It was a cold winter's day, 1st December 1995. She was walking along Wembley Central platform as she did from Mondays to Fridays after taking her son (then 18 months old) to the childminder and heading off to work in Maida Vale. The train was two minutes away from the station according to the earlier announcement made, and she was trying to get into the carriage that would stop closest to the exit where she would disembark the train.

Perlene heard a gentle voice calling out to her, and she looked to see who it was, thinking that it was someone she knew. Judas walked over to her and said hello politely and she whispered greetings back. As she said the word 'hi' she wondered to herself who this person was because she sure did not recognise him. The train pulled into the platform and they got on the same carriage together. They sat opposite each other and he began to ask her various questions; what is your name? Are you off to work?

Judas was on his way to sit his City and Guilds Electrical Installation exam at the time they met and he seemed friendly and so Perlene gave him her work number as he wanted to continue their conversation at some point in time. She got off the train before him and went to work as usual. However, she was facing many difficulties in her life at that time as she had resigned from her work a week earlier and was required to give a month's notice, so when she met Judas she had problems and needed someone to share them with.

Judas and Perlene started dating and they went out to the movies a few times and to dinner afterwards. He also took Perlene to meet his cousins and his uncle who he highly respected. Judas told the family of his intention to marry Perlene and they welcomed the news. The wedding plans were soon in progress and as both the couple were respected and loved by family and friends they volunteered to help with the arrangements and the expenses.

Judas and Perlene wasted no time to move in together and they were married seven weeks from the date they met. They got married on the 20th January 1996 and he moved into her flat in North West London where she lived with her two children at the time. It is her belief that Judas was her soul mate and they were destined to be together. It was as though they had known each other all their lives within the first week of meeting each other.

The wedding was planned over one month and the couple between them only had to buy the rings and the groom's suit. Friends and family gave generously. Perlene's mum bought her wedding dress, and made the wedding cakes; Judas' uncle hired a limousine car to transport the bride and groom to the registry office in Brent; Judas' best friend was his best man and he also rented a club for the reception to be held in Southall (The Tudor Rose); the caterers, champagne and wine was supplied by friends. One hundred and fifty guests were invited to the wedding and more attended. Perlene's daughter, Ahsiek, was flower girl and two of her sisters were bridesmaids.

The wedding was planned in a short time but was enjoyed by all who attended. They received so many gifts they had to share some with others. The one regret that Perlene had about her special day was that her sisters, Camille and Antoinette, did not attend.

Perlene found another job (soon after resigning from the one in Maida Vale). She found another job in Hammersmith, but with the encouragement of Judas, even though he was going through problems too, facing deportation back to Jamaica for overstaying whilst studying. Life finally began to piece together; the picture in the puzzle was beginning to take form. Immediately they started to plan ways of moving out of the flat and getting their own house. Both Perlene and her new husband paid the rent arrears she owed whilst being a single mum raising two children on her own. They decided to move closer to Perlene's mother who had moved to Middlesex a few years earlier. Perlene valued a closely-knit family unit and was particularly fond of her mother and loved having her living in close proximity to her.

Judas, after being together for 14 months and being married for 12 of those months, was deported back to Jamaica after trying to appeal against the decision to deport him for a period of two years. When Judas and Perlene first met he told her about his situation and she believed him because he showed her proof of the certificates he obtained whilst studying to become a qualified electrician and confirmation of that was the certificate he received for the exam he sat on the day they met which showed up through the post after passing first time. His intention was to return home to Jamaica if the appeal was rejected with his qualifications to enable him to seek employment there.

Perlene knew the risk that she took marrying Judas, but somehow it felt right and OK. She believed there was a future with him and that whatever happened they would somehow overcome and get on with their lives together. Judas left for Jamaica three weeks before she moved into their new home. He left home, that cloudy morning in February, to return to Jamaica, Perlene's heart broke and it took some time for it to mend. Perlene knew she had to continue what they started together, she was not going to let Judas down, and she was going to be a good and faithful wife to him. He was a good man and she was going to wait for him. The wait was long, hard and tiring but she did it with the help of her family, friends and God Almighty. She remained faithful even though she had an acquaintance enquiring whether she would wait for her husband or start a fresh relationship. She made a covenant with God to remain faithful to her husband so they would reunite after the three-year deportation order was revoked. Perlene believed they would survive the ordeal with all her heart.

Perlene visited Judas twice over the three year period and this was financially difficult as she had to take out more than one loan and credit card to help financially to care for her children and pay the bills. However, she kept the marriage alive by writing two or more letters to him each week. He called Perlene when he could and to be honest they were still as man and wife in many ways because whatever she was going to embark upon, whether change of employment or getting work done to the property they would discuss it and he would advise her about where to get help, get started and how to go about it.

Perlene joined a church in Wembley that she was introduced to by a very good friend (Jenny). She became very active in the church and so was very busy and knew that God was with her and family and she felt that he guided her too. There were times when she had financial hurdles and could see no way out but suddenly, with God's intervention through prayer, a solution to resolve the problem was found. Perlene being a Christian and having been baptised and converted in the Pentecostal faith since the age of 16, left the church through disobedience to follow her own desires away from the will of God until she came to the realisation that God was not just an image in her mind but he was also a personal friend who she could access at anytime spiritually. She walked by faith over the three years of being separated from Judas and her faith grew the more she found herself depending on God for solutions.

Finally Perlene's covenant with God materialised; well, being faithful to him reunited Judas and Perlene at long last the very same year that the deportation order was revoked. He had no difficulties in going to see the British High Commission in Jamaica after the three year period was up in February 2000. The millennium brought them joy and happiness because Judas was back in England, August 2000, and could have been back earlier if Perlene was able to pay for the flight sooner.

The day had arrived for his return and she waited patiently at the airport with a family member and Judas' cousin whom he highly respected. Perlene waited at the airport for a long time, and finally she saw him coming through arrivals. He looked thin but he was not well at the time, however. He greeted her casually and barely looked at her and went over to his cousin to greet him. She felt disappointed and wondered why he behaved in that way and her family member noticed too.

They left the airport and arrived home, where Judas got out and opened the front door of their new home. He looked pleased but as the house was not modernized, it was in need of refurbishment. But this could wait as now they were back together and things would change. Judas wasted no time finding employment and he began to work on the house almost immediately. However, Judas had changed in many ways and Perlene knew straight away that he was not the same man she had married.

It was not long before a son was born to the couple; Rad. Rad was born in August of 2001 so no time was wasted as by then Perlene was mid 30's and her biological clock was ticking away. Another son was born to them in 2003, Roy Junior, hence the family had now doubled. Having the boys was joyful and as Judas treated the other two children as his own, they were one big happy family.

Camille's Demon and Demise

Camille met a new partner after raising her boys as a single mum for a number of years. There were times when she suffered breakdowns and tried to take an overdose whilst raising them, but she always called for help when she took the tablets and her mother would call Antoinette and Perlene to assist. The extended family would all go to her home in the night to take care of the boys and one of them would accompany her to the hospital in the ambulance. She made two such attempts with her life, but no one knew exactly why she did it. Perlene felt being a single parent may have been hard to bear at times and so this was a cry for help. What Perlene did not realise is that there lurked several demons somewhere shut up inside Camille which she did not share with anyone from childhood.

Her new partner, Salohcin, moved in with her and her boys; he was new in her life and it was exciting times for her. He was tall and handsome, but also was not a one-woman man, which she later found out but he concealed this for years until eventually he persuaded her to move to East London which was quite a few miles away from her mother and sisters.

Camille was happy for a few years and the suicide attempts had stopped. However, she carried around the demons within her and did not share it with the family. She always wore a smile on her face; however, she was not afraid to show troublesome emotions. So if you did anything to offend her, you would soon know about it. She was known to throw a punch here and there when she felt it necessary.

The demon began to surface when she moved to East London and Salohcin began to show her what he was really capable of; he slept away when he wanted and did as he pleased within the relationship because he felt she had no one to help her now she had moved away from the locality of her extended family and so was vulnerable.

Camille fell pregnant with her third child and had a beautiful baby girl. Soon after giving birth she fell ill, and lost a lot of weight. She was now mentally impaired. Salohcin knew that she was not well but could not bear the thought of telling us that she needed help. However, she knew in her heart that her family would not turn her away if she went to them for help and so she decided to visit her mother when she began to hit rock bottom.

She moved to her mother in an unfit state to care for her then three children at the time. After much upset and debate she was taken into a hospital in Northwick Park where she lived for the next two years. Her mother took the children and was given custody of them through the courts. After a few months in hospital Camille realised she was pregnant with child number four. The child was for Salohcin and she gave birth to her in June 1998. Her mother took the baby home in the first week of her being born because Camille was unable to care for her.

It was through her hospital stay that Camille revealed her childhood demon, which she was haunted by before the age of 10. She was sexually abused by family members whom she should have been able to trust. Finally we understood why Camille tried to commit suicide on two occasions and why her life could not settle even though she tried hard. She was carrying a lot of baggage around and did not share it with the family because she felt ashamed (though it was through no fault of her own).

She felt unclean and hurt and Perlene believed that this was a daily occurrence in her life. She could not trust men because those she trusted abused her and perhaps those who really cared for her she could not trust anyway because her memories would not allow her to do so. Camille finally told the psychiatrist who was a consultant in the hospital where she resided about her demon that she kept a secret for over 15 years. The psychiatrist, with her permission consulted her mother, who immediately contacted the family members who were allegedly named by Camille to verify what was said.

Of course, as expected, each of them denied it, but now Camille could begin to heal, being that she was diagnosed as suffering from schizophrenia. Perlene believed her sister, and she truly was convinced that what Camille said was true. Perlene knew from her own experience. The problem here is that though she set her conscience free from the guilt of believing that she did something wrong and that she had no control over what happened to her, she felt that somehow her abused body had to be cleansed and a new body could then be formed. This belief sprung from her illness and to her it felt very real and possible.

Camille heard voices and they seem to control her emotions and actions. After two years she left the hospital and was eventually given a flat. She had found new friends whilst in the hospital, but the problem was that a few of them lived on the same ward as she did and were suffering from similar or worse mental conditions. Her social worker managed to house her close to where her mother lived so that she could have regular contact with her four children and her mother. Antoinette and Perlene were living in close proximity and so they would all meet up at their mother's home weekly.

Camille sometimes shared with Perlene what the voices told her. The most disturbing of the voices she heard was that which told her that she had to die in order to be reborn and then all that had happened to her would be history and she would be a new creation. When she shared this with Perlene, she tried her best to discourage the thought and cheer Camille up because Perlene felt her sister was feeling low at the time and that was how she called out for help. It appeared to have worked when she eventually smiled at Perlene's comforting words and she would then encourage Camille to take her medication because that would help her with the illness which provoked mood swings.

It was a Monday when the devastating phone call arrived via their mother whom Perlene could hardly hear over the phone. She was crying hysterically and after asking her to repeat herself, Perlene realised that it was the worst news anyone could get via a telephone call. The police had found Camille's body in her flat. She had injected herself with a fatal dose of a toxic substance over the weekend. Her body was found by a friend who alerted the police. The police visited their mother's home whilst she was alone and broke the news. Their mother called Perlene who immediately drove to her which took a maximum of 20 minutes to arrive.

The four children were now motherless, but her mother took care of them as they were already living with her. Finally, the most 'disturbing' voice succeeded, thought Perlene. This was so tragic for the family, but their loyalty to each other helped them to find solace at such a devastating time.

Camille's children ranked as priority now and they had to be protected and cared for in the early days of such a tragic time for the family. They knew that the family were there for them and what happened to their mum was unfortunate, but they had the assurance that they could go to grandma, Antoinette or Perlene for comfort and love. The main focus was to protect them and raise them up to be strong confident adults. History must not repeat itself ever again.

Antoinette's Joys and Sorrows

After Camille's funeral in December 2001, there was to be Antoinette's wedding in July 2002. There was much preparation leading up to the big day.

Antoinette by then had met her new intended husband and they had two daughters together. They had a total of four children in their family as both Antoinette and Howell had a daughter and son (respectively) from their past relationships. I guess 'after the darkness comes light' is a good way to describe their wedding which was needed to bring some joy and happiness after such sadness in their lives.

Perlene was to be Antoinette's maid of honour and it gave her some comfort to know that the youngest of the three was finally happy and had met her prince charming. Perlene's little freckle-faced baby sister was going to be wedded.

She truly deserved to be happy because she was hard working and ambitious. Whilst mourning the death of her sister in the midst of it all, she had her final exams for the AAT course and was still able to pass and qualify.

She was to marry a good man who was a friend, Perlene had met some years earlier at work. The moment he set eyes on Antoinette he vowed in his heart she was going to be his wife and from then he pursued her until he won her over and she was his bride.

The wedding was well organised and both bride and groom were born for each other. They remained the talk of the town for weeks after the wedding. The day was beautiful and the sun shone brightly in the sky until nightfall when they travelled to Europe for their honeymoon. They travelled together as Mr and Mrs for the very first time and the world was their oyster.

Tragedy was to strike early 2003 because the groom's mother died from a terminal illness only after being diagnosed short term. This was devastating to the family and Howell who was very close to his mother, struggled to deal with his loss. However, with the support of his wife and his extended family he coped as best as could be expected.

At the end of 2010 Antoinette's oldest daughter was pregnant with her first child. Antoinette felt concerned because her daughter was still completing her degree at university, so ideally she would have preferred her to finish her studies, get a job and make provisions for a new baby. Anyway, as is said, 'Why close the gate when the horse has already bolted?' A baby surely is a gift from God himself so has to be a good thing and a blessing.

Antoinette's joy was soon to turn to tragedy; disaster was to strike once again. Shante, her second child, suddenly collapsed on the field where she was competing in a cross country race; part of her unique feature was competing in competitive sports. She took part in cross country running as well as swimming competitions.

She died before she was transported to the hospital. She had great potential and was extremely intelligent. The greatest loss of all is that she was nearly14 years old and hadn't really had the chance to develop to her full potential which was very promising because she was going places. Antoinette suffered greatly at the loss of her daughter and trying to find answers is what kept both she and Howell in their right minds throughout this very sad and trying time. Their world suddenly turned upside down.

There was a hole in her heart that could not be filled and only time could help to sooth and heal it. 'Time is the master and God is the comforter'. Antoinette had not just suffered the loss of her sister, but now her beloved daughter, Shante, too. She was truly the most wonderful girl I knew with great potential ahead of her.

'Weeping may endure for a night but joy cometh in the morning.' Baby finally arrived in July 2011. The baby was honoured with the name of her late aunt, Shante. She was most gorgeous and Grandma Antoinette loves her dearly. She spends some of her spare time with her granddaughter who enjoyed the time with her grandmother also. Antoinette is quite funny and Shante enjoyed the games they play together such as 'peek-a - boo'.

God surely has ways of easing our sorrows and lightening our burdens when they seem to be unbearable.

Perlene's Childhood

Perlene spent nearly 14 years of her life living in Jamaica; nine of those years she grew up with her mother and the remaining time she lived with extended members of the family (her dad's aunt and her daughter).

Perlene can remember vaguely that her childhood was happy whilst her mother resided in Jamaica but then she left to join her sick mother in England with the promise to Perlene and her two sisters (Camille and Antoinette) to be reunited with her in the near future.

For the first two years after Perlene's mum migrated to England she had a happy life living with her dad's aunt, called Nut which was, of course, a pet name. One night Perlene went to bed and when she got up in the morning she was told 'Nut had a stroke' in the night and had to be admitted to hospital during the night. Perlene remembered visiting her in hospital but shortly after she died. Perlene loved Nut, as she showed her kindness and took care of her like she would her own grandchild.

When Nut died, her daughter Ecyoj continued caring for Perlene. She was not as kind but she made sure Perlene went to school and had food to eat. Perlene was an inherited responsibility to Ecyoj and this was clear to see. However, Perlene had ambition and held on to her mother's promise which was to send for her and her sisters or return to them.

At the age of three, Perlene developed epilepsy which was an embarrassing illness in her opinion to be labelled with, and she had to take medication daily in order to keep the sickness under control and get better. When Perlene had an epileptic episode she had no memory of what happened. She remembered that once she was conscious again there were either people standing around her with her mother crying in distress or she was in a car in the arms of her mother on the way to the hospital.

Perlene use to look forward to the summer holidays when her cousin whom she loved dearly, came over from the States to spend summer with the family (usually six weeks). Only then would she be given a bit of freedom to visit the countryside with Tricia where Tricia's father lived. Ecyoj was usually happy then because she would get money from Tricia's mother and other material things. Tricia also look forward to the holidays because a beauty contest was held each summer and of course Perlene never won as her outfits were never as gorgeous as Tricia's and as Tricia's brother was always the judge of the competition, well, his sister had to win.

Perlene never argued though as she never expected to win, and provided she was one on the runners up list (third place usually) she was happy. Perlene remembered that her younger cousin Delila cried at every beauty contest when she did not win and she would declare that the competition was fixed and unfair and screamed for all to hear her dissatisfaction. Well, Perlene believed Tricia was most beautiful and wore the best dresses so it was difficult for anyone to compete with her and she deserved to win.

One summer when Tricia came to Jamaica there was a power cut and so one of Ecyoj's friends from across the road volunteered to stay with the girls whilst she went to find candles.

He was a close friend of the family and he tried to touch Perlene inappropriately where he knew he should not and she told Tricia because she was not afraid to voice her opinion and sort him out. Tricia made a fuss and he left them both on their own and went back to his home. When Ecyoj got back they told her that his mother called him so he had to go. They never told her the real reason but he knew that he should never try anything like that again.

For a child, sexual abuse by an adult is shameful and so it is far easier to try and forget it and tell no one than to disclose it and run the risk of being called a liar or being looked upon in scorn as though you were to blame. At least this is what Perlene perceived in her mind and never took the initiative to behave otherwise.

I guess for Perlene, Tricia kept her safe and defended her without fear and that is why she was her guardian angel. Tricia knew more about Perlene than anyone else and knew she could disclose things that she kept dear to her heart without feeling vulnerable.

Perlene was beaten as a child and later realised that her bed-wetting problem continued due to the cruelty and the mental suffering that was imposed on her. She prayed for the day to come when her mother's promise would materialise and she would finally be reunited with her. Perlene knew she would never look back because there were many bad memories that haunted there in Kingston, Jamaica.

Perlene was to take the 11+ exam to go to high school; in Jamaica it was called Common Entrance Exams. Perlene's mother said she left hers and her sister's birth certificate with Ecyoj, but when Perlene had need for it so asked Ecyoj for it, she said she did not have it and that their mother did not give it to her. Perlene was unable to sit the exam without submitting her birth certificate to the examination board for entry so she had to settle for comprehensive high school which was the next alternative. Life was difficult but she was a survivor and never gave up. Perlene managed to stay in the higher tier class in high school and left to join her mother in year 8. She was an 'A' student (class 8A) but resources were limited.

Perlene's dream finally came through in June 1981 when she and her sisters joined their mother in England and life instantly changed for the good. Ecyoj did not help much in preparing the passage for the girls' journey. Instead, their father's mother; though not well, took the girls to the British High Commissioner and they were interviewed by a member of staff. At the end of the interview the entry visa was granted to all three girls, they received their visa to travel and finally light appeared at the end of the tunnel.

Perlene's childhood illness was about to come to an end. As soon as she was reunited with her mother, her bed-wetting problem ceased and the epileptic attacks ceased. She had a new life and a second chance to start all over again.

Perlene's Dream Shattered

Antoinette, Camille and Perlene dreamt of retiring and growing old together. The middle link of the chain had broken and the ultimate dream shattered in pieces and could not be put together again. How cruel is life? It swallows you, chews you up and then spits you out and of that, you have no control. Why should the beautiful roses whither and death have the final say?

England is a great place to live when the weather is good. However, when the weather is not so good, which is often, it makes you dream of the sunshine and the sea breeze cooling you down in the heat. Perlene dreamt of retiring back to Jamaica with her sisters when they got to retirement age. The dream was not meant to be. Once Camille had passed on, the dream ended.

Perlene dreamt of a home in Jamaica where she, Camille and Antoinette could finally live together and talk about their accomplishment, their past and look forward to the future things they would do together. At least that was the dream they had before they had families of their own.

Camille leaving so early left an empty gap with a void that could not be filled. There is emptiness and helplessness in that space that sits at the bottom of Perlene's heart that just won't budge. There are days when Perlene thinks about the conversations she used to have and the times they shared together. All she has left of Camille is her memories. She has children and Perlene can't help but look for her in them and to be honest, there are lots of her traits in them, especially the first girl.

Though Perlene was the eldest in age, Camille was the protector; she protected her sisters and would defend them in whatsoever way she could. She knew Perlene had a soft heart and would readily forgive rather than defend. Hence she would take matters into her hands when she felt that the culprit did not warrant forgiveness. She would position herself for battle, and woe unto those who were the trouble maker in her eyes. An example of this is where Perlene had a partner (Leoj) who kept cutting her external telephone wires which was situated outside her flat and because of this BT sent her a bill for the repairs carried out by their engineer to rectify the damage. Camille came to visit her whilst the maintenance engineer was outside the flat and when she learnt what was happening, she briskly went to the home of the offender, punctured one of his car tyres and then proceeded to give him a good beating outside his home.

The outcome of Camille taking such action put a stop to Leoj's unethical behaviour permanently and she never heard from him again. Camille was not one who started confrontations but she sure would finish it, if she felt there was a need.

Another incident where she defended Antoinette, whose dead-beat partner was cheating on her and refused to leave her flat so that she could move on with her life. Antoinette became upset when she learnt her partner was having an affair and asked him to leave but he refused so she rang her sister, Camille, and told her. Camille left her home with only one intention and that was to encourage the man who was giving her sister grief to leave instantly and that meant by force if that was the only solution. She got some black bags and packed his clothes in them and proceeded to put them at the front door of Antoinette's flat. She then called him and told him to pick them up before they either disappeared from the door or at worst was mistaken for rubbish by the refuse collection truck. Again this solved the problem as he called by to pick up the bags and bothered Antoinette no more.

Perlene still thinks about her a great deal; she was not just her sister but also her best friend because she could share secrets with her and Camille always took time to listen to her. Her love was genuine and she was there when you needed her. Even if you did not call her, somehow she would know you needed her.

Friends or Foes

Perlene as a child had just a few momentums to rekindle her childhood memories. She had no pictures of friends or souvenirs because she came from a poor background and could not afford luxuries such as a camera to capture precious moments. Pictures that most people had in their family albums were black and white and even the televisions that were in the more well-off families' homes were black and white. The television had one channel only so everyone watched the same programmes. Somehow those days were more satisfying because people socialised more, children played together outdoors and got more than enough exercise. Obesity was not a problem and food was fresh and more healthy options were encouraged because food was home grown and meat was bought fresh from the butchers within the local communities.

There was one item Perlene can remember that she wanted to take to England with her which was her Spanish school workbook, but she forgot it on top of the refrigerator in the kitchen, due to being overjoyed knowing she was leaving her, now, past behind. She never got it posted to her in England though she enquired about it on several occasions.

All Perlene took with her to England from her past was memories of her childhood. She could still remember friends she went to school with. She could remember her best friend in primary school who was mixed race (Chinese and Caribbean) whom she has tried desperately to locate but still has had no success in tracking her down. The other was in high school, who was mixed race (Indian and Caribbean). She still remembers their childhood faces, but has not been successful in her plight to find them. She is still very hopeful that one day she will accomplish this mission.

Perlene managed to locate one friend that she went to primary school with whom she once worked with and she hooked up with her on Facebook with a couple of other friends who are twins. Perlene remember them well but they couldn't remember her. However, she was in the year above them. She pursues trying to locate others on the website and hopefully someday she will.

Perelene has other friends in England whom she went to high school with and she still communicates with some of them. However, there is a still part of her who yearns for her early childhood friends. She realises that there are cultural differences with friends in England and though they communicate quite well she is unable to connect with them at grass root level.

Perlene lives in Middlesex and has done so for over 14 years; most of her friends live in North West London so she doesn't see them often. Thanks to mobile phones they are able to keep in touch regularly as people in general have busy lives.

Perlene's children attend school locally and so she managed to make new acquaintances through dropping and picking the boys up from school. However, it is not the same because she finds that she has difficulty in socialising as much as she would like, due to having the responsibility of raising a family and working part time. Usually when she gets a short break away for a weekend she enjoys accessing some alone time to enable the sustainability of herself. She takes this time to write, enjoy and explore nature.

In Perlene's 51 years of living on earth she has learnt to be observant of people. There are genuine friends and there are those who are around for a season only. Perlene has been hurt by friends more than once and she has had friends who are priceless. Perlene has had acquaintances whose sole intention was to use her for their own convenience and those who seek to release their baggage on her, to ease their own burdens.

As a child Perlene displayed leadership qualities and she was determine not to be a follower to those who were immoral and indisciplined. Perlene was able to detect and observe individuals by their attributes and so didn't allow those with parasitic or deceitful intentions to manipulate her good nature easily. Perlene tried very hard to stay in touch with genuine friends and those who are spiritually uplifting. She was a fairly good judge of character, so would usually realize sooner, rather than later the traits of the individual and their motive and decide whether it was worth the risk of letting the individual into her life.

Genuine friends tend to follow the motto 'do unto others as you would have them do to you'. Parasitic friends tend to overwhelm and flood you with requests and needed favours, yet they can never return them.

Perlene believes that life is a journey and to survive one has to safeguard oneself. To do this you need to be vigilant and observant. Wisdom is learnt but over time, growth is essential in this area and eventually the choices you make using your own wisdom will determine your path. Wisdom, in Perlene's opinion, contributes greatly to a self-fulfilled life.

An example of using wisdom is where her third child made friends with another boy in his class and this lead her to meeting the boy's parents. On a few occasions she dropped off and picked up the boy along with her own son to various events, so as to help because they had four children and the other three were younger.

The boy's father was genuine in helping Perlene with her son whereby if she got stuck at work or events he would return the favour by picking her boy up and vice versa. However, the boy's mother would ask for help even if it was not necessary and Perlene soon realised this and put an end to it as her expectation was not just as a friend but more of a dictator.

Perlene doesn't see her as a bad person, however, but she needs to acknowledge that her children are her responsibility and she needs to be aware that people will usually lend a helping hand when needed but won't be willing to take over her parental responsibility, especially when they do not deem it necessary. Perlene, being a mother of four, knew only too well.

Perlene's Omen

The phone rang and it was a friend of Perlene's daughter on the other end, Evemarie. She sounded angry and upset and of course Perlene was concerned about her anxiety. However, what Perlene was to learn that day was about to change her mood from being calm to being anxious because it changed her world permanently.

Evemarie, was annoyed at Perlene's daughter (Ahsiek) because she had not paid the gas bill and so owed her money to make the payment. Ahsiek was staying with Evemarie after leaving university within the 1st Semester of the first year of her Graphic Design degree. She did this because Perlene refused to agree to her leaving and returning home as she did not feel that Ahsiek was making the right decision.

Perlene was not aware of her daughter ever being dishonest with bill payments and so she questioned Evemarie further about the bill. Evemarie was standing beside her mother at the time listening to the conversation and she took the phone from her daughter, confirming to Perlene that her daughter was not lying and so Perlene offered to reimburse the money for the bill.

One conversation led to another and suddenly Evemarie's mother said to Perlene, "Have you noticed anything odd about your daughter?" Perlene asked her what she meant, thinking that the worst she could say was that Ahsiek was pregnant. Finally she said after pausing for a few seconds, that Ashiek was gay. Perlene heard what she said but it took a few moments for her brain to digest and absorb the information she had just been given by a stranger.

Perlene felt her heart sink deep into her chest and she was numb. She could not understand how her daughter could be gay and she had no idea. She lived at home with Perlene until she was 18 years old and she never saw the signs or detected anything unusual about her. Perlene politely thanked the woman for disclosing and sharing such sensitive information but she also felt humiliated on the other hand that a stranger had to disclose such private information about her own child to her.

The next few days were challenging and difficult for Perlene as she was faced with the dilemma of whether to approach Ashiek immediately or later. She was also worried about sharing such information within the family and extended family. She knew for sure that judgment was going to be made against her, being a Christian, and also her daughter whom she loved dearly. Disclosing this to anyone was a risk and also talking to anyone about it would indicate an acceptance of her daughter being gay before knowing for certain as she had not spoken to her to confirm whether this was true or not.

After a week had gone by Perlene plucked up the courage to discuss it with her husband and to her surprise and horror, he already knew. This was hard to bear and she could not stop crying for weeks. Her husband, Judas, was told by a family member and a friend that they saw Ashiek on two occasions at a gay club in the city, but he could not pluck up the courage to disclose it to her.

Perlene felt betrayed and she cried for days. She could not confront her daughter because she was hurting deep down inside. The pain was not just from hearing that Ashiek was gay but it was mainly from the betrayal, the deceit and the backbiting.

Those she loved and those she trusted caused her such emotional hurt and pain and to help her get over those emotions she had to pray fervently and forgive them which took her some time but she achieved her goal. She knew as a child of God she had to forgive everyone who knew and who did not tell her, because they all felt that they were protecting her by not letting her know. Perlene realised that she may have done the same to protect those she loved from emotional turmoil.

There was no easy way to disclose this information to a parent especially if they were ignorant of the subject matter. Perlene grew up amongst heterosexual people and was never exposed to gay people in her childhood or even as a teenager and so it was a shock to her.

After a few months went by Perlene rang her daughter and asked her if the rumour was true and Ahsiek confirmed that it was so, in tears. The odd thing is that though Perlene felt hurt, she still loved her, but there was a sigh of relief now as the matter was discussed between mother and daughter and they could both move on with their lives. Perlene was able to disclose to her daughter knowledge of how she felt and her daughter explained that it was difficult for her to disclose to Perlene her secret which she had kept for a number of years.

For other members of Perlene's extended family, they knew but no one talked about it because Ashiek has disclosed this on Facebook through her posted photos. Perlene spoke to her own mother about it and though she was not in favour, she still loved her granddaughter. However, she continued to pray for tolerance and deliverance. Perlene's eldest son knew also about his sister but he chosed not to discuss it.

Forgiveness

The meaning of forgive – cease to blame or hold resentment against (pardon); Collins Dictionary Thesaurus (reference).

Perlene found in the past that this is a popular topic, but is not one that is always easy to exercise. How does a parent forgive someone who murders, rapes or harms their precious gems (child/ren) especially when the act is unprovoked. St Mark 11 and verse 24 and 25 (King James Version of the Holy Bible) says "Therefore I say unto you, What things soever ye desire, when ye pray, believe that ye receive them, and ye shall have them. And when ye stand praying, forgive, if ye have ought against any: that your Father also which is in heaven may forgive you your trespasses".

We can see that forgiveness plays a very important part in our daily lives and without being able to carry out this act leaves us in limbo. Perlene experienced much unpleasantness, betrayal, deceit, unfaithfulness, etc., even at a tender age. There were various options that she could have chosen in life which meant that she would have lived in misery.

Relatives were a major cause to her emotional rollercoaster because of spoken words that were used recklessly. Words such as 'you will never amount to nothing', 'moon face girl', 'liar', 'piss up bed gal' and many others which would be rude to even repeat. Perlene was also epileptic as a child and so living on medication daily, she suffered side effects from the daily medication she was subjected to and these did not help towards her emotions.

She hated some of her relatives, but yet she yearned to be loved. There was one particular aunt that showed her love, who tried to protect her from cruelty and whilst she lived, Perlene was safe and felt protected. Her Aunt Nut would defend her if anyone tried to speak negatively against her. Some hated Perlene purely because she resembled her mother and she was not one they could push around and her mother made that very clear to her father's family. Being that Perlene was a 'carbon print' that duplicated her mother's looks, this sure was not embraced by her father's extended family.

When Aunt Nut died who was Perlene's carer after her mother travelled to England, the safety net was removed. The beauty of it all though is the more they tried to lower Perlene's self esteem and confidence, the more she was determined to prove them wrong. She was going to make something of her life and nothing except God himself was going to stop her. However, Perlene knew God loved her enough to help her to succeed in whatever path she chose along the way.

Perlene's first friend in England was a Christian (Pentecostal) and she was determine to introduce her to the man who loved her and gave his life for her, the man named Jesus, and it was not long after meeting her that Perlene got baptised.

Getting to know Christ helped people to forgive and it was then Perlene realised how much baggage she was carrying around. She had to forgive all of her relatives who had offended her and others who called her names and uttered bad things against her. Some were done in ignorance and some may have been done out of bitterness, but nevertheless she had to forgive them all so that she herself could receive forgiveness of her sins.

To forgive means that you have a better quality of life and most importantly peace. Not having peace means living in torment and that was too much for Perlene to bear. She practised forgiveness daily and once gotten into this routine, forgiveness became easier. Perlene deemed forgiveness necessary after living with people who find forgiveness very difficult to extend and as a result they became resentful towards others and often become bitter, hateful and untrusting.

The greatest penalty here would be that not being able to forgive others means that God cannot forgive us. Also our prayer request cannot be honoured either. Some of us may think forgiveness is a form of weakness but it is not. It simply means that we are human and we make mistakes and acknowledging that we make mistakes and acting upon this acknowledgement by forgiving others, releases us of those chains and thoughts that could further harm us and leave us in bondage. To forgive is honourable and shows humility.

Perlene's value life motto states that 'it is far easier to forgive and have peace and tranquillity than to be unforgiving and live in torment and misery'. We must remember that being able to forgive also teaches us how to be humble and show love.

The Beginning of the End for Perlene

Perlene's suspicion about her husband's, Judas', personality change was not wrong, as she strongly believed; observing his behavior at the airport the day he returned to England, He had begun to reveal his true character.

Judas deported back to Jamaica seemed to have taken its toil on the marriage. Whilst he and Perlene were apart, she wrote to him several times per month and shared most things with him. She was under the impression that he did the same, until they were reunited. Perlene fell pregnant in the same year Judas got back and they had a boy (Rad) and not long after that she fell pregnant again and had another boy (Roy Junior).

The children were hard work, being that there were four between them. Perlene had two children before they met. Life with four children wasn't easy but they provided for them the best way they could. The first two children accepted Judas as their father and as they were still young when they knew him, the girl (Ahsiek) being 9 and the boy (Matthew) was 18 months. They were young enough to adapt to such change. Judas showed them love and kindness so there was no known reason to doubt his genuine intentions.

Perlene's children had always meant a lot to her and she prided herself in being a good mother to them. As a child she had always felt love from her mother, and she never failed to tell Perlene, her beloved daughter, how much she loved her.

However, Perlene knew she loved her mostly by her actions because it was obvious. Perlene's mother left her at age 9 to join her biological mother in England, but before she departed she told Perlene that she would reunite with her and her sisters as soon as she could. It took five years but as soon as she got her residency in England she sent for them; her three girls together.

Perlene knew her mother's love and promise, so it was not hard for her to give these basic needs to her children. As the years went by the children grew up and Perlene's daughter first left home to attend university at age 19. Judas and Perlene began to drift apart slowly. The plan was to share their lives together and somewhere along the line Judas began to make plans for himself. He was the bread winner in the family so he felt that he did not have to share equal responsibility for the boys. When Perlene tried to work full time there was no support with the children because he told her that she should make all arrangements solely for them. Considering the type of attitude Judas had towards the family as a unit and the little support he gave, it was impossible for her to keep a full time job and look after a family. Sometimes Perlene had to work late and there was no one to collect the children from the after school club and so she had to give up full time employment.

Perlene tried self employment but again there were only so many hours she could put in as the children were still in primary school and had to be cared for. Perlene's career (accounts manager) suffered as a result and progression was slow, though she had no intention of giving up. Together Perlene and Judas began to gather worldly materials and as they progressed in so doing, 'us' became 'I'.

Judas now saw Perlene as a wife whose purpose in life was to attend to his needs and look after the children. He began to treat her shabbily. He tried continuously to lower her self esteem, but she fought back relentlessly. However, some days she felt exhausted and drained from the abusive verbal behaviour. The man she married had changed. She knew that had she not been a Christian who relied upon God for comfort, reading his words in the bible and developing a personal relationship with him she may have had a mental break down. She also had a strong mother who encouraged her to stand strong and fear not.

Perlene watched herself slowly deteriorating in caring for herself. She no longer took pride in self maintenance as she did before marrying Judas. She enjoyed looking good in her apparels and in turn it made her feel good. She started buying clothes that were unappealing and mostly dark colours. This was in the hope of hiding her existence. People began to talk and some kind friends would try to encourage her to pamper herself but at that time she had little disposable income and only had enough to spend on the children and the bills.

Judas stop taking her out and he talked about her behind her back; even at times whilst she was in the house, he spoke about her adversely to his friends who had visited. The worst thing about it was she knew and he knew that she heard the conversation but he did not care.

Perlene felt as though all her dreams were shattered knowing she had made great sacrifice to be with Judas and that she had never been unfaithful to him even though he had been unfaithful to her on more than one occasion. She knew she was no saint, but she was faithful to those she loved. From Perlene's experience she knew it was possible for someone you love to destroy you emotionally and bring you down to not even being worthy of being a door mat. There was a time she even began to talk to herself because she became so lonely with a lot of hurt shut up inside. She then realised that it was a thin line between sanity and madness. Eventually she began to talk to friends she worked with, who were also Christians and so it made conversations easier. The situation that was too 'big to tackle' was handled in prayer.

Just as she had thought things could not get worse, a ring went missing that belong to Judas in the house. He claimed he put the ring away in a particular place and it went missing. They searched for the ring but could not find it and he blamed Perlene's son (Matthew) saying that either he or his friends had taken the ring.

This caused a lot of doubt and cast a dark shadow over their already troubled family live. Matthew was never known to take anything from the house without first receiving permission. Perlene felt bitterness in her heart towards Judas and she was in limbo with her emotions as to whether Matthew would have taken the missing ring or not. Her mind wanted her to believe he took it but her heart wouldn't let her.

A few months after the ring went missing Perlene's wedding ring went missing too; however, she had great concerns and was saddened because the ring belonged to her grandmother who had long been deceased. That was all she possessed that belong to her grandmother and it was given to her by her own mother 30 years earlier.

Perlene's mind questioned both Judas and Matthew taking the ring. She felt if taken by Judas, it may have been to teach her a lesson of how he felt when Matthew took his ring (allegedly) and if it was Matthew, it was to take revenge for being blamed for something he did not do. Also Perlene's heart was telling her she had placed it somewhere and forgot where she left it. Her heart was right because as sure as after the night cometh the day, she did place it somewhere and forgot as she so realised, when she found the ring in the skirt pocket she was wearing the very day the ring went missing.

Judas later progressed to having an affair with Perlene's cousin in their marital home and marital bed. He was not sorry for what he did and never admitted to her that he did so.

She knew he had a sexual relationship with Delila because one of the most common errors men make when they cheat on their partner is to try to convince their partner that the other woman they are cheating with is gay in order to cover up their actions and intentions. Her husband did not realise that this gave his secret away by making it more apparent.

However, Perlene's cousin was a regular visitor in their home, as she visited in the summer holidays and after she left the summer of 2011, Judas's ring went missing. This caused turmoil in their home for a year. However, the ring suddenly showed up Summer 2012 when she was making her annual visit once again and the idea of the 'missing ring' was conjured up to cause upset in the family, giving Judas a perfect reason to leave his family for her.

However, God had another plan that revealed all and so it was not as simple as they thought it was going to be because Perlene certainly did not deserve it.

Bye Bye Grandma May

It was the month of August when the mobile phone went off; the number was showing up as overseas. Perlene wondered who was on the other end because the number was not one she recognised. She answered the call and heard her aunt's (father's sister) voice on the other end; it was dreadful and sad news. "May died yesterday in hospital," said Aunt Doreen. Perlene paused for a moment to digest what she had just heard.

She knew that the phone call would one day arrive but hoped that it would not be for a few years yet. This meant travelling to the U.S.A (Newark) for the funeral. Grandma May was the last of her generation to pass on. She was her beloved grandmother whom she trusted and adored. She had lived to the age of 87 and had enjoyed a full life. At the time she passed away she had six children, 12 grandchildren and 23 great grandchildren. She knew all of them and loved all too.

Grandma May was the only living relative Perlene could depend on to discuss the family history, going back from her great grandmother and grandfather who came from Montego Bay in Jamaica (West Indies). Though she had aged, physically her long-term memory was extraordinary. She even retained memories from her childhood. It was a joy to sit and hear the many stories she had to tell about Perlene's early childhood years.

Sadly, Grandma May lost a child at an early age that she never forgot and spoke about her as though it only happened yesterday. Grandma May lost a granddaughter (Camille) and a great granddaughter (Shante) also.

Grandma May raised her children in Jamaica but later they all migrated to the United States of America. She outlived all her siblings even though she was not the youngest. Grandma May's eldest son was Perlene's father (Abe) and her first grandchild was Perlene.

Funerals means gathering of relatives and family and though it is good for the family to have reunions, it can also be difficult because of the occasion and the event. Perlene left her children and husband behind to travel to Newark, though feeling sad, somewhat looking forward to seeing relatives she hadn't seen for years.

The Delila Saga

It has been a long summer for Perlene especially because the visitor started to show her true colours.

Perlene, being an hospitable person, has always opened her door every summer to her cousin who resides in Newark, but unknown to her, she was plotting against her. She had willingly allowed the snake to crawl into her home and maybe even her bed. The adversary had her plans but little did she know that it would backfire.

Perlene confided in her cousin Delila and shared confidential family matters with her. However, what she did not know was that the information was used as a weapon to move in on her territory.

It was a sunny afternoon in July when Perlene sat down with Delila making conversation. Perlene was pouring out her heart to her about confidential family matters. After sometime into the conversation she began to realise that Delila was taking the side of a particular family member in his defence. She was not interested in hearing both sides and continued to make remarks against Perlene. Perlene began to wonder why this was happening and where the conversation would lead. A few days later another conversation between cousins took place, again Perlene began to notice that once again she could not do anything right. The longer the conversation took place, the more negative Delila grew towards Perlene.

For many summers, Delila visited and Perlene had no reason to suspect any foul play or negativity. Perlene's suspicion was aroused when Delila began to attack her verbally when she spoke about her Christian belief. This was a bit of a shock because all the family knew that Perlene was a Christian and had been for many years. It was common news. Delila clearly made it known that she did not believe that God existed and had no intention to have any form of conversation that he did. Perlene started to be fearful because she felt that a person who did not believe or ever perceived that there was a higher being than themself who governed over us, was capable of doing anything, even committing murder, as they probably had no conscience or moral standards.

The sad thing about this particular summer was that Perlene's grandmother, who also lived in Newark, died. She was devastated that her grandmother had passed away and she had not been able to see her before she died. Unfortunately Delila was away too, in Europe, at the time and had to return to Newark before her vacation was over for the funeral.

Delila was sad being she had to go early because she had plans up her sleeve that were about to come to an end and as Perlene was now aware that there was foul play, she kept a close watch on both partners in crime to avoid them making any further silly mistakes that could have been fatal for all involved, including Perlene and her children. About six weeks before Delila had to return to Newark, she was admitted to the hospital claiming that she had terrible bleeding caused by fibroids. However, from everything that went on that summer, there could have been a possibility of miscarriage rather than fibroids, but of course it is only an opinion.

Here I could say that Perlene's belief as a Christian could have its rewards because it is said 'What's done in the dark must come to light' and if there was foul play between both parties then maybe this was one way to proclaim that there is really a higher being that is greater and who puts 'wrongs' right.

Perlene suffered by the hands of those she loved and still managed to stand as she was forewarned in dreams previous to her ordeal. The upside in this was that Perlene grew stronger because she overcame this challenge in her life. She also learned to be more cautious with those around her and not to let her guard down as carelessly, as it could have detrimental consequences. A new motto she grasped from this experience was 'Everyone is guilty until proven innocent' and she comforted herself in remembering that some lessons are learnt the hard way.

Emotional Turmoil

"I do", they are no easy words. Whilst the love flows those words are like honey to the ears but when love turns to hate the vows are like bitter herbs when taken forcibly as medicine. How do you mend together the pieces of a broken heart? Where do you begin? This is a true test of the mind; it separates the rational from the emotional way of thinking. There were days that the sun never shone and the rain of bitterness continued to trickle down her spine; oh how the pain lingered endlessly.

Perlene became blinded with anger and frustration and she so wanted to find relief and happiness. In her pursuit she threw herself in the arms of her ex-lover and it was a temporary solution but was far from the one she really needed. It was like 'going from the frying pan into the fire'. He was on a mission and she was vulnerable and lonely.

Samson (ex-lover) studied psychology at university level so knew how to embark upon his mission to trap his victims. Perlene, though vulnerable, was not exactly totally naïve. However, she knew that she could not allow herself to fall head over heels in love with a 'player', but nevertheless comfort and lustful desires needed to be fulfilled.

Spring had just sprung, when Perlene got a phone call from Samson; his voice had not changed over the years she had known him, and it sounded sweet and melodious as it ever did. That voice sounded so calm and inviting and though it was a short conversation, there were plans to meet the very next day.

After the first meeting and Samson explaining what he had been doing with his life and the places he had been, Perlene and Samson reminisced about their past relationship and what could have been. The evening went by quickly and Perlene knew this was going to be the beginning of more than friendship. They became 'friends with benefits' and those benefits included lust, sex and the toppings.

The friendship went well, despite the many lies and deceit that were conjured up, but the passion compensated and paid for that negative behaviour in full, signed, sealed and delivered. Perlene having experienced Samson's behaviour patterns in the past knew more or less what he was capable of so she was not surprised when she witnessed nail prints that were freshly made on his back and unanswered phone calls and explanations that made no sense whatsoever (example – "I don't know where those nail prints came from but what I do know is that some strange supernatural occurrences have been happening to me when I go to bed at nights"). Perlene knew that really there was no real commitment and Samson was free to do what he liked, but somewhat he felt it was best to explain rather than say nothing at all.

Samson helped Perlene to set up her business and assist her in whatever area she needed help without complaint and so given these factors he was really the best friend she had though she never admitted that to him.

Samson at the time was going through a divorce of his own and also needed support from Perlene and so the relationship was good and necessary for both parties involved.

Perlene's children enjoyed Samson's company as he would take them to football and other places of leisure. He got on well with them also but unfortunately Perlene's eldest child and

Samson did not see eye to eye and that caused disagreements and arguments at times.

Perlene and Samson remain friends to this very day but as one would put it 'too much, too little, too late'.

Milestone in Perlene's Life

As a young girl Perlene was determined to succeed in whatever conquest she pursued; she had set goals and had no intentions of failing any. You see, for Perlene, giving up meant never being able to try again but provided she was given the opportunity to have another go at it, well there was light at the end of the tunnel. Perlene was diagnosed with epilepsy at the age of three. She was being transported on her father's bike, holding on to his waist sitting at the rear of it when the bike met into an accident and she fell off the bike. She fitted and as a result, contracted the paralytic illness as she so described.

Perlene's mother, being protective over her girls, had decided that she would take care of Perlene for the rest of her life as she could not be sure that her daughter would be capable of taking care of her personal needs as a result of her condition. As Perlene got older the illness became a curse to her as it was embarrassing when she had the attacks and regained consciousness. She would usually fall to the floor and have no recollection of the experience she had encountered but she would notice people standing around her and at times her mother would be crying and calling for help to get Perlene to the hospital.

The seizures meant that Perlene had to be monitored regularly by the hospital and was on daily medication which was administered to her three times a day until she could do so by herself. She had limited friends in primary school (Kingston,

Jamaica) as children did not understand the condition and so preferred not to keep friends with her. Some parents were also superstitious so they instructed their children to refrain from playing with Perlene. They felt that Perlene was possessed by an evil spirit and that she could cause harm to their children.

For Perlene, life was not fair but she comforted herself to know she had siblings who did not bother about her illness and played with her without reservations. At age almost 14 years, when Perlene migrated to England, her mother, knowing that Perlene was diagnosed with epilepsy at an early age, took her to the doctors who referred her to get tested at a hospital in Maida Vale (London). How ecstatically overjoyed she felt when the test revealed that there was no trace of the sickness and that she was completely cured of the antisocial ailment. She was epilepsy free at last, no longer to be plagued by the awful stigma that was assigned to it. Surely this was a miracle worth rejoicing over!

This meant that her secondary school life was going to be different; she did not have to explain the 'evil' to any of her new friends that she was going to make at her new school. Her mother would no longer have to worry about her not being able to live an independent life.

Though Perlene had epilepsy she did not allow this to stop her learning ability; in fact, it was quite the opposite. As a result of having to spend a lot of time alone, she read books and did her homework as well as extra curriculum work in primary school and so made the top classes in her primary school years as well as the first two years in secondary school. In Jamaica children are grouped into class according to their academic ability and for a child with epilepsy they were not expected to aspire to 'A' classes. The grading system was from A-F. A child in F was failing whilst a child in 'A' class would be performing academically at the highest level acheivable.

Perlene started at 'E' grade in primary school and left primary school at level 6 grade A. So that is class 6A. She left Jamaica whilst in class 8A, which shows in terms of knowledge that she was performing at the highest possible level in her year.

Life in Jamaica was not easy because children at age 9 years were taught how to wash their clothes by hand and were given daily chores to complete which had to be done without excuses. If those chores were not done then discipline was imminent and sometimes those punishments that were used as a deterrent, were quite harsh. Perlene was quite petrified of being beaten with the tamarind switch or the belt. However, being a child who was prone to making mistakes as is expected, there are times when Perlene would fail to complete her task in the allotted time and so had to face the consequence.

Epileptic episodes would sometimes arise from such punishments and this could mean that Perlene would end up in the hospital as an outpatient. The upside to this is that Perlene would be pampered and receive special treatment whenever she was unwell and had one of her seizures.

Most of Perlene's teenage life was the same as many other teenagers in the Western world who arrived in England from the West Indies. Being the eldest of now six children as the family had extended due to her mother being married and having three more children, making a total of six, Perlene had to assist in caring for her siblings.

The new additions included another two girls (Adole and Lorraine) and one boy (Anthony). Perlene enjoyed her role as second in charge after her parents and she was mature enough to help organise and see to the smooth running of the home. Her mother worked full time in a hospital as an auxiliary nurse, doing shift work and so she had to help with caring for her siblings. Perlene was sensible and was always keen to learn.

Looking after younger siblings was not new to Perlene as she did this in Jamaica for Camille and Antoinette, being the eldest child, so she expected to help anyway. Her mother's husband, now her new dad, was an honourable man in her eyes as he cared for her and her sisters more than their own biological father ever did. So, helping around the house was a polite way to show gratitude and appreciation.

Life wasn't always a bed of roses for Perlene; she watched her parents struggle to put food on the table and to care for them all. She had plans to get a good education to enhance her own life; she did not want to struggle as her parents did and she had to set a good example for her younger siblings to follow so that their lives could be better too.

At the age of 15 years old Perlene found her first job on her own, though there were times she did random work for friends and family. She found employment in Woolworths two months before her 16th birthday and she was given a sales assistant position. The job was only for Saturdays at first as she was still in full time education. That was to pave the way in terms of gaining work experience and obtaining a good reference to move onto greener and more prestigious pastures.

Perlene's employment history includes: dry cleaning, factory worker, department store sales assistant, working with an artist, financial advisor for an advertising agency, book keeper for an estate agent, junior accountent for a property management company, management accountant fr a glass company, trainee accountant for an accountancy firm, accounts manager and director of her own company etc.

Perlene's present role is a childminder and she embarked upon this career when she decided to work from home. As explained earlier, Perlene engaged in caring roles from a tender age (childhood) and gained considerable amount of experience in this area so she felt she could pursue a career as a childcare practitioner, utilising her skills and knowledge in caring for children and working with parents to achieve the full potential in their cognitive ability to support them in their development as ethical and confident individuals.

Perlene's First Love

It was a Saturday night when Perlene was at a party with some friends. Her best friend Urtha joined her on a girls' night out. The music that was being played at the time was 'Lover's Rock' which was predominantly played at most teenage party/clubs in the 1980's. How we rocked to that music; even if one could not dance, they could move to the rhythm of the beat. Well that was never a problem for Perlene who would buy the latest apparels in fashion to attend those parties in style. Though Perlene enjoyed the music and the groove she did not smoke and only drank alcohol when she was staying overnight sparingly as she was very in tune with her health and safety, ensuring that she could give an account for her actions and encounters the day after.

As Perlene stood near the entrance door of the club she notice a tall, slim handsome guy peering at her. She pretended not to notice but couldn't help glancing now and again to be sure he was still eyeing her. Finally he approached her and introduced himself as one of the DJ's who was entertaining that night. Perlene spoke with him apprehensively with few words as she didn't want to give an impression that she was an easy catch. They danced a couple of times during the evening and exchanged numbers in the hope that one of them would make the call. Well, you guessed it, Perlene did not make the first call; Drew did call the very next day. He invited her to another party he was hosting and she went along with Urtha and some other friends.

To cut a long story short they eventually got together as a couple and months later Perlene fell pregnant. Perlene having strong Christian values had every intention of keeping her child, but for Drew the relationship was moving too quickly. Drew was 21 years old and Perlene was age 18. The relationship was soon to become strenuous for the couple, Drew was into entertainment and had access to many female friends and acquaintances and so it wasn't long before he started cheating on Perlene who was still pursuing her studies.

Before Ashiek was born the relationship had ended but Drew was given access to see the baby. Perlene was going to be second to none and she was not willing to share a man with another woman because she did not feel she had to. She took a year's break from full-time studies to look after her baby girl and returned to college to complete level 1 of the ACCA (accounting qualification). The duration of the course was one year and she successfully finished it, with distinction.

Perlene decided to delay going to university for two years whilst she worked full time to save the money for the fees and also to accumulate enough funds to maintain her baby and herself. She worked for Dorland's Advertising Agency in London, Paddington for two years in their accounts department and in that time applied to attend Thames Valley University in Ealing. She successfully got onto the course and completed her degree in two years rather than three. She obtained an honours degree in Finance and Accounting in 1993. Perlene's ambition in life to succeed steered her in the direction of progress.

Whilst completing her degree she passed her driving test and bought a MG Metro second-hand car to help with transporting her child and herself with a bit of ease to help her manage her daily tasks. Perlene's mother assisted her in quite a number of ways, helping her to care for Ashiek and gave some financial support when she could. Perlene had her own apartment whilst studying so she had to pay the rent and bills too. She worked part time for Harrow Council doing home care to help with finances at the time.

Perlene graduated and her mother, father and daughter attend the graduation. She felt proud as she had achieved a major set goal.

Perlene Jump From the Frying Pan into the Fire

Perlene had now started another era in her life; she found employment with an accountancy firm (Bridger Smart) in West Drayton where she got an opportunity to practise accountancy, putting her knowledge into use. She met Samson whilst attending church and they became friends in the first instance. He seemed a decent respectable person and Perlene grew to love him but Perlene once again was to regret such a decision.

Samson was softly spoken and always made time to visit and go places with Perlene. They shared a lot of interest together such as church, university education, cultural background, etc. But unknown to Perlene, Samson shared similar and intimate interests with other female who were just as gullible as Perlene at the time.

Samson was able to deceive many women. He was so professional at what he did that he covered his tracks very carefully and none of us knew about the other. Though his stories were a bit suspicious at times, somehow he would be able to cover them and you would actually believe the stories he conjured up. Perlene was in a make-belief relationship with Samson for four years and within that time frame they had a child together (Matthew), Samson got married secretly to someone else and due to noticeable and obvious changes in his behavior, it became apparent that something wasn't quite right. So Perlene began to make enquiries and watched him closely and she then learnt that he now had a wife. She ended the relationship with Samson and moved on with her life. Being the deceiver he was, the marriage ended within two years.

For Perlene, being a single parent with two children was no easy life. She faced many challenges along the journey. There were uncountable barriers and obstacles to overcome. These difficulties helped Perlene to mature and her fighting instincts encouraged her to continue moving as there was certainly light at the end of the tunnel.

Perlene was living in Kilburn (North West) London when Matthew was born. Ahsiek, being age seven years, was in primary school, and attended school in Harrow where her mother lived at the time, because she would drop and pick her up from school to help Perlene with childcare cost which was quite expensive for single parents to afford.

Perlene did not expect to end up with two children who were fatherless because she felt she and Matthew's father could have made it together and that eventually they would marry. This was not to be so she had continued the struggle the best she could. Perlene worked hard so that she could buy her home and move closer to her mother and to where her daughter attended primary school. She got a better paid job and with the help of a housing association she was able to buy her house in Hayes, Middlesex. She purchased half from the housing association, whilst renting the other half until she was able to buy the property in full.

Perlene got married to Judas in the process of trying to buy a house but Judas was deported back to Jamaica before the purchase was completed. Therefore, he was unable to help financially, hence why the housing association assisted her.

Perlene moved to Hayes in March 1997, the same year Judas was deported and the same year Lady Diana died.

The move to Hayes, a new community, meant Perlene had a fresh start to raise her family. She soon got familiar with the local shops and social clubs. She got to meet new people when her children started school there. The people were welcoming, especially her neighbours who were elderly people but very pleasant in their personality. They were a form of guardian angels in Perlene's life as they would support her in more ways than one. This included when she had to visit her deported husband in Jamaica over a three-year time period whilst he was away; they would keep a watch on the property and pop over to make sure that all was well.

Confident Little Emeralds

Perlene, after 15 years of residing in Hayes, decided to further educate herself as a childcare practitioner. She completed a course and required procedure to register as a childminder offering a service that was carried out in her home to the local community. Her boys, Roy Junior and Rad, were both still at school and she felt it would benefit the family for her to work from home, embarking on a career that she loved and was passionate about.

The rise in knife crimes also made her nervous; the crime rate was growing considerably and this was predominantly amongst young black teenage boys. She wanted to be a supportive parent to her children and wanted to be at home when they returned from school rather than them getting home to an empty unsupervised home in the cold winter's evening.

Perlene started her new career in 2015 and her business grew quite quickly which was a blessing in disguise as she had just gotten divorced so was faced with financial difficulties and with the threat of her home being repossessed. Perlene was not going to sit back and do nothing; she was prepared to work hard to keep her children in their home as they had already been through enough adverse situations, witnessing numerous arguments between their parents.

The children she cared for in her childminding business ranged from age between 10 months to13 years. These children she treated no differently from her own children, showing them love and due care. Her setting was diversified and children of various cultures, religious backgrounds and of special needs were catered for to a high standard. Children who left the settings and moved into primary school and other countries never forgot Perlene. They would text, phone or even visit her on occasions, especially at Christmas and Easter.

On Perlene's 50th birthday, as a gift to Perlene, one of the children who had migrated to Barcelona invited Perlene to spend time with his family in their family home when they were settled and his parents took time off work to escort Perlene around Barcelona. Perlene's holiday included flight, accommodation and food which were paid for in full by the child's parents. The parents were so pleased with the job Perlene did working in partnership with them to help care for their son that they felt they wanted to show their appreciation.

There was another family of two boys whom she cared for, dropping and picking them up from school and those boys had been in the care of other local childminders but once they started to attend her setting they were comfortable and so had no intentions of moving on to any other childminder because in their own words they proclaimed they had never met a childminder who offered a service which made them feel as though they were members of her family. On her 50th birthday they took her to their favourite restaurant in Southall and on occasions they invited Perlene to their home to join them for family meals.

Perlene did her job to the best of her ability and this was appreciated by the parents as they felt their children were in safe hands when they were left in her care.

Friends with Benefits

Perlene's bad luck with the choice of men in her life had been an area that she had failed to conquer. She just did not know how to choose the right partner; at least one that was compatible. Perlene's long lasting dream was to have a partner who could share her interest. She wanted a companion who shared her sense of humour. The inner Perlene had an almost childlike desire to be accepted for who she was as a person. She did not want to be stereotype or perceived to be who she was not.

Perlene knew that due to the many disappointments in her life starting from her early childhood, trust was not something which she found easy to freely give; she always had reservations when she met new people. She was always very sceptical of them at first; from her experience, actions speak louder than words. To truly get to know a person it was better to rely on their behaviour which reflects their true character rather than taking their word as gospel.

She would almost always expect the opposite sex to let her down in one way or another. When she met Drew, he told her he loved her, which could not have been the case judging by his actions. She later met Samson who told her what he felt she wanted to hear, but her experience with him was even more painful than that with Drew. Finally she met Judas, her ex-husband who though their marriage lasted for 19 years, was deceitful and evil in her own opinion.

Perlene is convinced that there must be someone out there in the universe for her but with all that she has experienced in life being a single parent once again with four children, she is not prepared to take the risk presently to venture into a relationship with the intention of marriage until her boys have grown into adulthood.

'Friends with benefits' is a temporary solution but this could also have adverse effect as emotions can begin to take over and one could end up suffering emotional distress. Being in a marriage for such a long duration has its attachments, but when one thinks of the pain, suffering and anxiety when going through a divorce that often helps to subdue sexual desires.

Perlene has had a few dreams of getting married again. She knows that her encounter in these dreams makes her feel good. Her dream husband seems to possess that which she seeks in an ideal relationship but also seems to have a resemblance of someone she has met before but just can't remember when or where.

Only time will determine whether this dream is supernaturally real or just something hoped for. However, regardless of the outcome it is good for one to have faith. For now, Perlene will make do with a dream that will one day mature.

I guess for Perlene this would be a new and exciting chapter for her. She dreams of travelling to those countries she has not yet visited, but with a partner who would enjoy so doing. She enjoys reading romantic novels as they keep her imagination spiralling and her dreams alive.

Back to Jamaica

In 1994 Perlene finally landed in Kingston Jamaica for the first time after leaving with her sisters in 1981. As she stepped down from the glistening steps of the aircraft onto the authentic Jamaican soil, she smiled. However, the heat was fierce and she soon felt the humidity and suddenly remembered that this was the land of her birth. As she went through customs there was a power cut which lasted for about a minute or so but seemed at the time to be much longer which made Perlene a little fearful as she was not sure what was happening. The emergency light came on and Perlene could breath freely once again.

Airports were never her favourite place as there are some gruesome stories in the media about them being hijacked. That was not in Perlene's holiday plans so she would not have prepared an escape plan just in case!

Perlene stayed with a family friend who picked her up from Norman Manley Airport in Kingston. The journey to her home in Spanish Town was long but the meal that was awaiting Perlene was worth the travel. The table was spread with ackee and saltfish (Jamaica's national dish) with boiled yam and green banana with fresh vegetables and not forgetting the East Indian mango, star apple and coconut jelly with a cool glass of lemonade.

The holiday was enjoyable for Perlene and she visited relatives whom she had not seen for over 13 years. Most of her relatives, including her father and grandmother, had migrated to America so there were only a few cousins left behind.

The sandy beaches were adorable and she basked in the sun, drinking coconut water and eating fried fish. The food was lovely and fresh and the surroundings were inviting and welcoming. People in Jamaica are quite friendly but there are some areas that are not recommended to visitors and returning citizens and so should be avoided.

The community where Perlene lived with her aunt before she left for England was not very safe for visitors to venture into as they did not like strangers including Perlene, as she had lived abroad for a considerable amount of time and so her face was unfamiliar to many. To venture into that locality without the assistance of someone who already lived there would be dangerous and so people avoided going there for their own safety.

Perlene took her daughter (first child) with her on the vacation. Ahsiek enjoyed the visit but the sun was very hot and so she complained about the heat. Perlene regularly applied sun lotion to protect her daughter from sunburn. The main visit to Jamaica was to visit her mother's grandmother who was still alive (Perlene's great grandmother). Mammy was in her 90s and still had good vision, could hear well, speak well and recognise Perlene too. They spoke for hours and Perlene, being the first of the family in England to return to Jamaica for a holiday, this was appreciated by Mammy. Ahsiek was able to see her twice great-grandmother (being she was now Mammy's fifth generation). This was historical for both Perlene and her daughter because Mammy died a couple of years later.

Mammy's Legacy

Mammy was born in the early 20th century and had siblings, mostly sisters, but due to poverty she did not receive an education. She had more than one children but Perlene's grandmother was the only surviving child. Mammy raised her daughter well, who later got married to Perlene's grandfather. They had children together including Perlene's mother (Grandma Phil), but they were later divorced.

Mammy's daughter left for England in the 1960s and left behind, her six children including Perlene's mother (Anrol). Grandma Phil left Jamaica to join her new husband with the intention to settle in her new residence and then send for the children. Unfortunately, that was not to be as Anrol being one of the older siblings was to learn that her mother's new husband refused to sign the legal papers required by immigration for them to gain entry to join their mother in England.

This was certainly a disappointment for the children who now had to find alternative ways of survival because their grandmother was not young enough to work full time and also she had to look after the six children that were left behind. Anrol loved her Grandmother Mammy very much and would try to help with the younger siblings the best she could. She did odd jobs here and there to help out financially at a young age and was unable to finish secondary school due to hardship.

Grandma Phil did the best she could to maintain her children left behind but her funds were limited. However, she did the best she could to support them. This is a prime example of children left behind with their grandparents in the West Indies with the hope that one day they would reuntie with their family who left Jamaica to settle abroad. Disappointment struck when they were to learn differently that this was not to be the case.

Anrol did not let this news stop her from achieving her goals, though they were more difficult to access and would take more time to achieve. Anrol met Perlene's father in her teenage years and they had a family of their own. They had Perlene, Camille and Antoinette. They moved in together to raise their family but after some years Anrol finally got the opportunity to travel to England to join her mother who was terminally ill and requested that her daughter joined her in England to help administer her medication and to give her daily injections.

It is not an easy process to invite adult children to join their parents in England unless the circumstance is exceptional. This request had passed that test and so, although Anrol felt gutted to leave her three girls behind, she made the sacrifice for her dying mother. This was to be the only opportunity for Anrol to spend time with her mother whom she had not seen for over 15 years and loved dearly. She found comfort in knowing that she would reunite with her girls again one way or another.

Grandma Phil lived for a further three years with the care of her daughter Anrol who looked after her well. Anrol was able to do some cleaning work whilst caring for her mother. The jobs did not pay much but she sent maintenance home for her girls every month as well as the occasional barrels with clothes and food for them. Anrol was determine to look after her three girls because she remembered as a child that her dreams were shattered because of broken promises.

When Grandma Phil died Anrol got married as she did not have the time to form relationships whilst looking after her terminally-ill mother. She got leave to remain in England soon after and she was then able to work full time and send for her girls to join her in England. Her husband signed the legal papers for the girls to join them without any difficulty but she made it very clear to him that if he had any objections in so doing, she had no choice but to return to Jamaica to look after her daughters.

Anrol had no intentions of returning to her daughters' father in Jamaica because though they lived together, he had habits that she could not live with and the major one was gambling. Gambling was everything to him and this controlled his finances which was a parasite in many ways as this uncontrollable habit destroyed countless relationships and families.

Anrol worked long hours looking after her family and she did this with joy because she knew that she was able to achieve for her children what her parents could not do for her and her siblings. She had other children from her marriage and she raised them well. She certainly was fulfilled because the promise she made to her daughters when she left Jamaica was honoured and all of her children finished full time education and went on to further their studies in colleges and universities. God had answered her ultimate prayers.

Perlene's Biological Father (Abe)

Abe never got over the fact that Anrol moved on with her life. He always believed that she would come back to him and so this was hard to accept when he learnt that she was married and had more children. Abe's heart was broken but he learnt to live with that fact.

After the girls left to join their new family, Abe met someone whom he later got married to and started a new family of his own. His new wife gave birth to two sons and they all migrated from Jamaica to America to join his mother (Grandma May) who filed for him and his siblings.

Abe sought employment in New York and worked as a chef for a number of years. He corresponded with Perlene and her sister via telephone conversations. In the summer time, Perlene and her sisters took turns in visiting their father and brothers.

In discussions with her dad, Perlene realise that he had always kept a spark in his heart for Anrol as he loved her dearly and believed she was his soul mate but he felt life had dealt him a cruel blow when she left for England and never returned to him.

Tania Arrives

It was the beginning of spring in 1983 when Anrol brought a large box which she carried in her hands and placed it down on the kitchen floor. There was a noise coming from inside the box that sounded like barking. Perlene quickly opened the box whilst Camille and Antoinette stood peering at the box and Anrol waited quietly to see the look on the girls' faces when they opened up the box. Inside the box was a cute little black puppy with brown spots on her face. She was adorable and Perlene and her sisters gave her the name Tania. Tania knew how to entertain the family; she would follow Perlene and her sisters up the stairs to their bedrooms and when they hid under the sheets, she would find them and bark at them.

On several occasions the children got into trouble because they would make excessive noise that would disturb the neighbours and so they would complain, so Anrol would terminate the game and give the girls a warning and if they failed to adhere, they would be punished.

Tania had puppies of her own and though Perlene and her sisters protested against Anrol giving the puppies to the local pet shop, they lost the battle as her words were final. The local pet shop was about five minutes away so Perlene went to visit the puppies until they were all sold which did not take very long as they were lovely puppies.

On one occasion Lorraine pulled Tania's tail and she tried to stop her by barking at her. Loraine hit at thwe dog and the dog's teeth accidently caught the tip of one of her fingers so Lorraine, in a rage, turned around, grabbed the dogs tail and bit it. Tania knew she was only a toddler at the time so she did not hurt her; instead she whimpered and walked away from her. Anrol gave her time out so she could think about her action.

Tania had the puppies with the neighbour downstairs' (maisonette) dog; he was a Labrador and his name was Glen. Anrol decided to move to Harrow as the family had outgrown their home and so unfortunately Tania had to separate from Glen. They never saw each other again and two years after the move Tania died. The vet said it was from sunstroke but Perlene believed it was from heartbreak.

Perlene's Hobby

Perlene at a young age loved singing; she had inherited good vocals from her mother. She attended vocal classes and even had the opportunity to sing at the Apollo in her teenage years. Perlene joined the choir at church and there she was able to do what she loved doing best. She sang at various events and sometime sang solo. Perlene used her voice as a way of expressing her emotions, singing according to her moods. She would sing 'the blues' when she was feeling low and sings 'Lovers Rock' when she was in love. Music allowed Perlene to express herself; even as a child when she felt lonely she would sing those songs that would perk up her spirit, such as *I am leaving on a jet plane*.

Singing is therapeutic and gives a sense of belonging. Perlene long mastered the heart of relaxation through this therapy. Maturing in age has expanded her interests to include classical music which she appreciates especially at those very anxious and stressful times in her life.

Perhaps sometime in the future Perlene will finally produce an album doing what she loves best and sharing this with those she loves.

Life for Perlene continues and who knows where it may lead. However, for Perlene she has experienced enough to write a novel sharing her experiences which may be **valuable** to others. In a world where we know not what lies ahead, we must venture in faith knowing that we have been assigned our purpose, which must be fulfilled and hope that when we finally depart from this life, our mission is fully accomplished.